# *If I Should Die*

---

## Rupert Brooke

A Phoenix Paperback

This abridged edition published in 1996 by Phoenix
a division of Orion Books Ltd
Orion House, 5 Upper St Martin's Lane, London WC2H 9EA

Cover illustration: Photograph of Rupert Brooke (Hulton Deutsch
Collection)

ISBN 1 85799 656 9

Typeset by Deltatype Ltd, Ellesmere Port, Cheshire
Printed in Great Britain by
Clays Ltd, St Ives plc.

# Contents

## Fragment

I strayed about the deck, an hour, tonight
Under a cloudy moonless sky; and peeped
In at the windows, watched my friends at table,
Or playing cards, or standing in the doorway,
Or coming out into the darkness. Still
No one could see me.

                 I would have thought of them
– Heedless, within a week of battle – in pity,
Pride in their strength and in the weight and firmness
And link'd beauty of bodies, and pity that
This gay machine of splendour 'ld soon be broken,
Thought little of, pashed, scattered. . . .

                    Only, always,
I could but see them – against the lamplight – pass
Like coloured shadows, thinner than filmy glass,
Slight bubbles, fainter than the wave's faint light,
That broke to phosphorus out in the night,
Perishing things and strange ghosts – soon to die
To other ghosts – this one, or that, or I.

## The Dance

### A Song

As the Wind, and as the Wind,
   In a corner of the way,
Goes skipping, stands twirling,
Invisibly, comes whirling,
Bows before, and skips behind,
   In a grave, an endless play –

So my Heart, and so my Heart,
   Following where your feet have gone,
Stirs dust of old dreams there;
He turns a toe; he gleams there,
Treading you a dance apart.
   But you see not. You pass on.

# 1914

### 1. Peace

Now, God be thanked Who has matched us with His hour,
 And caught our youth, and wakened us from sleeping,
With hand made sure, clear eye, and sharpened power,
 To turn, as swimmers into cleanness leaping,
Glad from a world grown old and cold and weary,
 Leave the sick hearts that honour could not move,
And half-men, and their dirty songs and dreary,
 And all the little emptiness of love!

Oh! we, who have known shame, we have found release
  there,
 Where there's no ill, no grief, but sleep has mending,
  Naught broken save his body, lost but breath;
Nothing to shake the laughing heart's long peace there
 But only agony, and that has ending;
  And the worst friend and enemy is but Death.

## II. *Safety*

Dear! of all happy in the hour, most blest
    He who has found our hid security,
Assured in the dark tides of the world that rest,
    And heard our word, 'Who is so safe as we?'
We have found safety with all things undying,
    The winds, and morning, tears of men and mirth,
The deep night, and birds singing, and clouds flying,
    And sleep, and freedom, and the autumnal earth.

We have built a house that is not for Time's throwing.
    We have gained a peace unshaken by pain for ever.
War knows no power. Safe shall be my going,
    Secretly armed against all death's endeavour;
Safe though all safety's lost; safe where men fall;
And if these poor limbs die, safest of all.

### III. *The Dead*

Blow out, you bugles, over the rich Dead!
   There's none of these so lonely and poor of old,
    But, dying, has made us rarer gifts than gold.
These laid the world away; poured out the red
Sweet wine of youth; gave up the years to be
   Of work and joy, and that unhoped serene,
    That men call age; and those who would have been,
Their sons, they gave, their immortality.

Blow, bugles, blow! They brought us, for our dearth,
   Holiness, lacked so long, and Love, and Pain.
Honour has come back, as a king, to earth,
   And paid his subjects with a royal wage;
And Nobleness walks in our ways again;
   And we have come into our heritage.

## IV. *The Dead*

These hearts were woven of human joys and cares,
   Washed marvellously with sorrow, swift to mirth.
The years had given them kindness. Dawn was theirs,
   And sunset, and the colours of the earth.
These had seen movement, and heard music; known
   Slumber and waking; loved; gone proudly friended;
Felt the quick stir of wonder; sat alone;
   Touched flowers and furs and cheeks. All this is ended.

There are waters blown by changing winds to laughter
And lit by the rich skies, all day. And after,
   Frost, with a gesture, stays the waves that dance
And wandering loveliness. He leaves a white
   Unbroken glory, a gathered radiance,
A width, a shining peace, under the night.

## v. *The Soldier*

If I should die, think only this of me:
    That there's some corner of a foreign field
That is for ever England. There shall be
    In that rich earth a richer dust concealed;
A dust whom England bore, shaped, made aware,
    Gave, once, her flowers to love, her ways to roam,
A body of England's, breathing English air,
    Washed by the rivers, blest by suns of home.

And think, this heart, all evil shed away,
    A pulse in the eternal mind, no less
        Gives somewhere back the thoughts by England given;
Her sights and sounds; dreams happy as her day;
    And laughter, learnt of friends; and gentleness,
        In hearts at peace, under an English heaven.

## The Treasure

When colour goes home into the eyes,
   And lights that shine are shut again,
With dancing girls and sweet birds' cries
   Behind the gateways of the brain;
And that no-place which gave them birth, shall close
The rainbow and the rose: –

Still may Time hold some golden space
   Where I'll unpack that scented store
Of song and flower and sky and face,
   And count, and touch, and turn them o'er,
Musing upon them: as a mother, who
Has watched her children all the rich day through,
Sits, quiet-handed, in the fading light,
When children sleep, ere night.

## Tiare Tahiti

Mamua, when our laughter ends,
And hearts and bodies, brown as white,
Are dust about the doors of friends,
Or scent a-blowing down the night,
Then, oh! then, the wise agree,
Comes our immortality.
Mamua, there waits a land
Hard for us to understand.
Out of time, beyond the sun,
All are one in Paradise,
You and Pupure* are one,
And Taü, and the ungainly wise.
There the Eternals are, and there
The Good, the Lovely, and the True,
And Types, whose earthly copies were
The foolish broken things we knew;
There is the Face, whose ghosts we are;
The real, the never-setting Star;
And the Flower, of which we love
Faint and fading shadows here;
Never a tear, but only Grief;

* Tahitian for 'fair', the name given to himself.

Dance, but not the limbs that move;
Songs in Song shall disappear;
Instead of lovers, Love shall be;
For hearts, Immutability;
And there, on the Ideal Reef,
Thunders the Everlasting Sea!

    And my laughter, and my pain,
Shall home to the Eternal Brain.
And all my lovely things, they say,
Meet in Loveliness again;
Miri's laugh, Teïpo's feet,
And the hands of Matua,
Stars and sunlight there shall meet,
Coral's hues and rainbows there,
And Teüra's braided hair;
And with the starred *tiare's* white,
And white birds in the dark ravine,
And *flamboyants* ablaze at night,
And jewels, and evening's after-green,
And dawns of pearl and gold and red,
Mamua, your lovelier head!
And there'll no more be one who dreams
Under the ferns, of crumbling stuff,
Eyes of illusion, mouth that seems,
All time-entangled human love.
And you'll no longer swing and sway
Divinely down the scented shade,

Where feet to Ambulation fade,
And moons are lost in endless Day.
How shall we wind these wreaths of ours,
Where there are neither heads nor flowers?
Oh, Heaven's Heaven! – but we'll be missing
The palms, and sunlight, and the south;
And there's an end, I think, of kissing,
When our mouths are one with Mouth . . .


   *Taü here*, Mamua,
Crown the hair, and come away!
Hear the calling of the moon,
And the whispering scents that stray
About the idle warm lagoon.
Hasten, hand in human hand,
Down the dark, the flowered way,
Along the whiteness of the sand,
And in the water's soft caress,
Wash the mind of foolishness,
Mamua, until the day.
Spend the glittering moonlight there
Pursuing down the soundless deep
Limbs that gleam and shadowy hair,
Or floating lazy, half-asleep.
Dive and double and follow after,
Snare in flowers, and kiss, and call,

With lips that fade, and human laughter,
And faces individual,
Well this side of Paradise! . . .
There's little comfort in the wise.

## Retrospect

In your arms was still delight,
Quiet as a street at night;
And thoughts of you, I do remember,
Were green leaves in a darkened chamber,
Were dark clouds in a moonless sky.
Love, in you, went passing by,
Penetrative, remote, and rare,
Like a bird in the wide air,
And, as the bird, it left no trace
In the heaven of your face.

In your stupidity I found
The sweet hush after a sweet sound.
All about you was the light
That dims the greying end of night;
Desire was the unrisen sun,
Joy the day not yet begun,
With tree whispering to tree,
Without wind, quietly.
Wisdom slept within your hair,
And Long-Suffering was there,
And, in the flowing of your dress,
Undiscerning Tenderness.

And when you thought, it seemed to me,
Infinitely, and like a sea,
About the slight world you had known
Your vast unconsciousness was thrown. . . .

O haven without wave or tide!
Silence, in which all songs have died!
Holy book, where hearts are still!
And home at length under the hill!
O mother-quiet, breasts of peace,
Where love itself would faint and cease!
O infinite deep I never knew,
I would come back, come back to you,
Find you, as a pool unstirred,
Kneel down by you, and never a word,
Lay my head, and nothing said,
In your hands, ungarlanded;
And a long watch you would keep;
And I should sleep, and I should sleep!

## The Great Lover

I have been so great a lover: filled my days
So proudly with the splendour of Love's praise,
The pain, the calm, and the astonishment,
Desire illimitable, and still content,
And all dear names men use, to cheat despair,
For the perplexed and viewless streams that bear
Our hearts at random down the dark of life.
Now, ere the unthinking silence on that strife
Steals down, I would cheat drowsy Death so far,
My night shall be remembered for a star
That outshone all the suns of all men's days.
Shall I not crown them with immortal praise
Whom I have loved, who have given me, dared with me
High secrets, and in darkness knelt to see
The inenarrable godhead of delight?
Love is a flame: – we have beaconed the world's night.
A city: – and we have built it, these and I.
An emperor: – we have taught the world to die.
So, for their sakes I loved, ere I go hence,
And the high cause of Love's magnificence,
And to keep loyalties young, I'll write those names
Golden for ever, eagles, crying flames,
And set them as a banner, that men may know,

To dare the generations, burn, and blow
Out on the wind of Time, shining and streaming. . . .
These I have loved:

        White plates and cups, clean-gleaming,
Ringed with blue lines; and feathery, faery dust;
Wet roofs, beneath the lamp-light; the strong crust
Of friendly bread; and many-tasting food;
Rainbows; and the blue bitter smoke of wood;
And radiant raindrops couching in cool flowers;
And flowers themselves, that sway through sunny hours,
Dreaming of moths that drink them under the moon;
Then, the cool kindliness of sheets, that soon
Smooth away trouble; and the rough male kiss
Of blankets; grainy wood; live hair that is
Shining and free; blue-massing clouds; the keen
Unpassioned beauty of a great machine;
The benison of hot water; furs to touch;
The good smell of old clothes; and others such –
The comfortable smell of friendly fingers,
Hair's fragrance, and the musty reek that lingers
About dead leaves and last year's ferns. . . .

                        Dear names,
And thousand other throng to me! Royal flames;
Sweet water's dimpling laugh from tap or spring;
Holes in the ground; and voices that do sing;
Voices in laughter, too; and body's pain,
Soon turned to peace; and the deep-panting train;
Firm sands; the little dulling edge of foam

That browns and dwindles as the wave goes home;
And washen stones, gay for an hour; the cold
Graveness of iron; moist black earthen mould;
Sleep; and high places; footprints in the dew;
And oaks; and brown horse-chestnuts, glossy-new;
And new-peeled sticks; and shining pools on grass; –
All these have been my love. And these shall pass,
Whatever passes not, in the great hour,
Nor all my passion, all my prayers, have power
To hold them with me through the gate of Death.
They'll play deserter, turn with the traitor breath,
Break the high bond we made, and sell Love's trust
And sacramented covenant to the dust.
– Oh, never a doubt but, somewhere, I shall wake,
And give what's left of love again, and make
New friends, now strangers. . . .
                                    But the best I've known
Stays here, and changes, breaks, grows old, is blown
About the winds of the world, and fades from brains
Of living men, and dies.
                                    Nothing remains.

Oh dear my loves, O faithless, once again
This one last gift I give: that after men
Shall know, and later lovers, far-removed,
Praise you, 'All these were lovely'; say, 'He loved.'

## Fafaïa

Stars that seem so close and bright,
Watched by lovers through the night,
Swim in emptiness, men say,
Many a mile and year away.

And yonder star that burns so white,
May have died to dust and night
Ten, maybe, or fifteen year,
Before it shines upon my dear.

Oh! often among men below,
Heart cries out to heart, I know,
And one is dust a many years,
Child, before the other hears.

Heart from heart is all as far,
Fafaïa, as star from star.

## Waikiki

Warm perfumes like a breath from vine and tree
   Drift down the darkness. Plangent, hidden from eyes,
   Somewhere an *eukaleli* thrills and cries
And stabs with pain the night's brown savagery;
And dark scents whisper; and dim waves creep to me,
   Gleam like a woman's hair, stretch out, and rise;
   And new stars burn into the ancient skies,
Over the murmurous soft Hawaian sea.

And I recall, lose, grasp, forget again,
   And still remember, a tale I have heard, or known,
An empty tale, of idleness and pain,
   Of two that loved – or did not love – and one
Whose perplexed heart did evil, foolishly,
A long while since, and by some other sea.

## One Day

To-day I have been happy. All the day
   I held the memory of you, and wove
Its laughter with the dancing light o' the spray,
   And sowed the sky with tiny clouds of love,
And sent you following the white waves of sea,
   And crowned your head with fancies, nothing worth,
Stray buds from that old dust of misery,
   Being glad with a new foolish quiet mirth.

So lightly I played with those dark memories,
Just as a child, beneath the summer skies,
   Plays hour by hour with a strange shining stone,
For which (he knows not) towns were fire of old,
   And love has been betrayed, and murder done,
And great kings turned to a little bitter mould.

## A Memory

### (From a sonnet-sequence)

Somewhile before the dawn I rose, and stept
   Softly along the dim way to your room,
   And found you sleeping in the quiet gloom,
And holiness about you as you slept.
I knelt there; till your waking fingers crept
   About my head, and held it. I had rest
   Unhoped this side of Heaven, beneath your breast.
I knelt a long time, still; nor even wept.

It was great wrong you did me; and for gain
Of that poor moment's kindliness, and ease,
And sleepy mother-comfort!
                Child, you know
How easily love leaps out to dreams like these,
Who has seen them true. And love that's wakened so
Takes all too long to lay asleep again.

## Clouds

Down the blue night the unending columns press
  In noiseless tumult, break and wave and flow,
  Now tread the far South, or lift rounds of snow
Up to the white moon's hidden loveliness.
Some pause in their grave wandering comradeless,
  And turn with profound gesture vague and slow,
  As who would pray good for the world, but know
Their benediction empty as they bless.

They say that the Dead die not, but remain
  Near to the rich heirs of their grief and mirth.
    I think they ride the calm mid-heaven, as these,
In wise majestic melancholy train,
  And watch the moon, and the still-raging seas,
  And men, coming and going on the earth.

## There's Wisdom in Women

'Oh love is fair, and love is rare;' my dear one she said,
'But love goes lightly over.' I bowed her foolish head,
And kissed her hair and laughed at her. Such a child was
    she;
So new to love, so true to love, and she spoke so bitterly.

But there's wisdom in women, of more than they have
    known,
And thoughts go blowing through them, are wiser than
    their own,
Or how should my dear one, being ignorant and young,
Have cried on love so bitterly, with so true a tongue?

## He wonders whether to Praise or to Blame Her

I have peace to weigh your worth, now all is over,
    But if to praise or blame you, cannot say.
For, who decries the loved, decries the lover;
    Yet what man lauds the thing he's thrown away?

Be you, in truth, this dull, slight, cloudy naught,
    The more fool I, so great a fool to adore;
But if you're that high goddess once I thought,
    The more your godhead is, I lose the more.

Dear fool, pity the fool who thought you clever!
    Dear wisdom, do not mock the fool that missed you!
Most fair, – the blind has lost your face for ever!
    Most foul, – how could I see you while I kissed you?

So . . . the poor love of fools and blind I've proved you,
For, foul or lovely, 'twas a fool that loved you.

## Mutability

They say there's a high windless world and strange,
  Out of the wash of days and temporal tide,
  Where Faith and Good, Wisdom and Truth abide,
*Æterna corpora*, subject to no change.

There the sure suns of these pale shadows move;
  There stand the immortal ensigns of our war;
  Our melting flesh fixed Beauty there, a star,
And perishing hearts, imperishable Love. . . .

Dear, we know only that we sigh, kiss, smile;
  Each kiss lasts but the kissing; and grief goes over;
  Love has no habitation but the heart.
Poor straws! on the dark flood we catch awhile,
  Cling, and are borne into the night apart.
  The laugh dies with the lips, 'Love' with the lover.

## The Funeral of Youth: Threnody

The day that *Youth* died,
There came to his grave-side,
In decent mourning, from the county's ends,
Those scatter'd friends
Who had lived the boon companions of his prime,
And laughed with him and sung with him and wasted,
In feast and wine and many-crown'd carouse,
The days and nights and dawnings of the time
When *Youth* kept open house,
Nor left untasted
Aught of his high emprise and ventures dear,
No quest of his unshar'd –
All these, with loitering feet and sad head bar'd,
Followed their old friend's bier.
*Folly* went first,
With muffled bells and coxcomb still revers'd;
And after trod the bearers, hat in hand –
*Laughter*, most hoarse, and Captain *Pride* with tanned
And martial face all grim, and fussy *Joy*,
Who had to catch a train, and *Lust*, poor snivelling boy;
These bore the dear departed.
Behind them, broken-hearted,
Came *Grief*, so noisy a widow, that all said,

'Had he but wed
Her elder sister *Sorrow*, in her stead!'
And by her, trying to soothe her all the time,
The fatherless children, *Colour*, *Tune*, and *Rhyme*,
(The sweet lad *Rhyme*), ran all-uncomprehending.
Then, at the way's sad ending,
Round the raw grave they stay'd. Old *Wisdom* read
In mumbling tone the Service for the Dead.
There stood *Romance*,
The furrowing tears had mark'd her rougèd cheek;
Poor old *Conceit*, his wonder unassaug'd;
Dead *Innocency's* daughter, *Ignorance*;
And shabby, ill-dress'd *Generosity*;
And *Argument*, too full of woe to speak;
*Passion*, grown portly, something middle-ag'd;
And *Friendship* – not a minute older, she;
*Impatience*, ever taking out his watch;
*Faith*, who was deaf, and had to lean, to catch
Old *Wisdom's* endless drone.
*Beauty* was there,
Pale in her black; dry-eyed; she stood alone.
Poor maz'd *Imagination*; *Fancy* wild;
*Ardour*, the sunlight on his greying hair;
*Contentment*, who had known *Youth* as a child
And never seen him since. And *Spring* came too,
Dancing over the tombs, and brought him flowers –
She did not stay for long.
And *Truth*, and *Grace*, and all the merry crew,

The laughing *Winds* and *Rivers*, and lithe *Hours*;
And *Hope*, the dewy-eyed; and sorrowing *Song*; –
Yes, with much woe and mourning general,
At dead *Youth's* funeral,
Even these were met once more together, all,
Who erst the fair and living *Youth* did know;
All, except only *Love*. *Love* had died long ago.

## The Way that Lovers Use

The way that lovers use is this;
   They bow, catch hands, with never a word,
And their lips meet, and they do kiss,
   – So I have heard.

They queerly find some healing so,
   And strange attainment in the touch;
There is a secret lovers know,
   – I have read as much.

And theirs no longer joy nor smart,
   Changing or ending, night or day;
But mouth to mouth, and heart on heart,
   – So lovers say.

## The Night Journey

Hands and lit faces eddy to a line;
    The dazed last minutes click; the clamour dies.
Beyond the great-swung arc o' the roof, divine,
    Night, smoky-scarv'd, with thousand coloured eyes

Glares the imperious mystery of the way.
    Thirsty for dark, you feel the long-limbed train
Throb, stretch, thrill motion, slide, pull out and sway,
    Strain for the far, pause, draw to strength again. . . .

– As a man, caught by some great hour, will rise,
    Slow-limbed, to meet the light or find his love;
And, breathing long, with staring sightless eyes,
    Hands out, head back, agape and silent, move

Sure as a flood, smooth as a vast wind blowing;
    And, gathering power and godhead as he goes,
Unstumbling, unreluctant, strong, unknowing,
    Borne by a will not his, that lifts, that grows,

Sweep into darkness, triumphing to his goal,
    Out of the fire, out of the little room! . . .
– There is an end appointed, O my soul!
    Crimson and green the signals burn. The gloom

Is hung with steam's fantastic livid streamers.
　　Lost into God, as lights in light, we fly,
Grown one with will, end-drunken huddled dreamers.
　　The white lights roar; the sounds of the world die;

And lips and laughter are forgotten things.
　　Speed sharpens; grows. Into the night, and on,
The strength and splendour of our purpose swings.
　　The lamps fade; and the stars. We are alone.

## Home

I came back late and tired last night
  Into my little room,
To the long chair and the firelight
  And comfortable gloom.

But as I entered softly in
  I saw a woman there,
The line of neck and cheek and chin,
  The darkness of her hair,
The form of one I did not know
  Sitting in my chair.

I stood a moment fierce and still,
  Watching her neck and hair.
I made a step to her; and saw
  That there was no one there.

It was some trick of the firelight
  That made me see her there.
It was a chance of shade and light
  And the cushion in the chair.

Oh, all you happy over the earth,
  That night, how could I sleep?
I lay and watched the lonely gloom;
  And watched the moonlight creep
From wall to basin, round the room.
  All night I could not sleep.

## The Chilterns

Your hands, my dear, adorable,
  Your lips of tenderness
– Oh, I've loved you faithfully and well,
  Three years, or a bit less.
  It wasn't a success.

Thank God, that's done! and I'll take the road,
  Quit of my youth and you,
The Roman road to Wendover
  By Tring and Lilley Hoo,
  As a free man may do.

For youth goes over, the joys that fly,
  The tears that follow fast;
And the dirtiest thing we do must lie
  Forgotten at the last;
  Even Love goes past.

What's left behind I shall not find,
  The splendour and the pain;
The splash of sun, the shouting wind,
  And the brave sting of the rain,
  I may not meet again.

But the years, that take the best away,
   Give something in the end;
And a better friend than love have they,
   For none to mar or mend,
   That have themselves to friend.

I shall desire and I shall find
   The best of my desires;
The autumn road, the mellow wind
   That soothes the darkening shires,
   And laughter, and inn-fires.

White mist about the black hedgerows,
   The slumbering Midland plain,
The silence where the clover grows,
   And the dead leaves in the lane,
   Certainly, these remain.

And I shall find some girl perhaps,
   And a better one than you,
With eyes as wise, but kindlier,
   And lips as soft, but true.
   And I daresay she will do.

## Love

Love is a breach in the walls, a broken gate,
    Where that comes in that shall not go again;
Love sells the proud heart's citadel to Fate.
    They have known shame, who love unloved. Even then
When two mouths, thirsty each for each, find slaking,
    And agony's forgot, and hushed the crying
Of credulous hearts, in heaven – such are but taking
    Their own poor dreams within their arms, and lying
Each in his lonely night, each with a ghost.
    Some share that night. But they know, love grows colder,
Grows false and dull, that was sweet lies at most.
    Astonishment is no more in hand or shoulder,
But darkens, and dies out from kiss to kiss.
All this is love; and all love is but this.

## It's not going to Happen Again

I have known the most dear that is granted us here,
    More supreme than the gods know above,
Like a star I was hurled through the sweet of the world,
    And the height and the light of it, Love.
I have risen to the uttermost Heaven of Joy,
    I have sunk to the sheer Hell of Pain –
But – it's not going to happen again, my boy,
    It's not going to happen again.

It's the very first word that poor Juliet heard
    From her Romeo over the Styx;
And the Roman will tell Cleopatra in hell
    When she starts the immortal old tricks;
What Paris was tellin' for good-bye to Helen
    When he bundled her into the train –
Oh, it's not going to happen again, old girl,
    It's not going to happen again.

## The Busy Heart

Now that we've done our best and worst, and parted,
  I would fill my mind with thoughts that will not rend.
(O heart, I do not dare go empty-hearted)
  I'll think of Love in books, Love without end;
Women with child, content; and old men sleeping;
  And wet strong ploughlands, scarred for certain grain;
And babes that weep, and so forget their weeping;
  And the young heavens, forgetful after rain;
And evening hush, broken by homing wings;
  And Song's nobility, and Wisdom holy,
That live, we dead. I would think of a thousand things,
  Lovely and durable, and taste them slowly,
One after one, like tasting a sweet food.
I have need to busy my heart with quietude.

## Song

The way of Love was thus.
He was born, one winter morn,
With hands delicious.
And it was well with us.

Love came our quiet way,
Lit pride in us, and died in us,
All in a winter's day.
There is no more to say.

# *Song*

All suddenly the wind comes soft,
    And Spring is here again;
And the hawthorn quickens with buds of green,
    And my heart with buds of pain.

My heart all Winter lay so numb,
    The earth so dead and frore,
That I never thought the Spring would come,
    Or my heart wake any more.

But Winter's broken and earth has woken,
    And the small birds cry again;
And the hawthorn hedge puts forth its buds,
    And my heart puts forth its pain.

## *The Old Vicarage, Grantchester*

Just now the lilac is in bloom,
All before my little room;
And in my flower-beds, I think,
Smile the carnation and the pink;
And down the borders, well I know,
The poppy and the pansy blow . . .
Oh! there the chestnuts, summer through,
Beside the river make for you
A tunnel of green gloom, and sleep
Deeply above; and green and deep
The stream mysterious glides beneath,
Green as a dream and deep as death.
– Oh, damn! I know it! and I know
How the May fields all golden show,
And when the day is young and sweet,
Gild gloriously the bare feet
That run to bathe . . .
                              *Du lieber Gott!*

Here am I, sweating, sick, and hot,
And there the shadowed waters fresh
Lean up to embrace the naked flesh.
*Temperamentvoll* German Jews                     41

Drink beer around; – and *there* the dews
Are soft beneath a morn of gold.
Here tulips bloom as they are told;
Unkempt about those hedges blows
An English unofficial rose;
And there the unregulated sun
Slopes down to rest when day is done,
And wakes a vague unpunctual star,
A slippered Hesper; and there are
Meads towards Haslingfield and Coton
Where *das Betreten*'s not *verboten*.

ειθε γενοίμην . . . would I were
In Grantchester, in Grantchester! –
Some, it may be, can get in touch
With Nature there, or Earth, or such.
And clever modern men have seen
A Faun a-peeping through the green,
And felt the Classics were not dead,
To glimpse a Naiad's reedy head,
Or hear the Goat-foot piping low: . . .
But these are things I do not know.
I only know that you may lie
Day-long and watch the Cambridge sky,
And, flower-lulled in sleepy grass,
Hear the cool lapse of hours pass,
Until the centuries blend and blur
In Grantchester, in Grantchester. . . .

Still in the dawnlit waters cool
His ghostly Lordship swims his pool,
And tries the strokes, essays the tricks,
Long learnt on Hellespont, or Styx.

Dan Chaucer hears his river still
Chatter beneath a phantom mill.
Tennyson notes, with studious eye,
How Cambridge waters hurry by . . .
And in that garden, black and white,
Creep whispers through the grass all night;
And spectral dance, before the dawn,
A hundred Vicars down the lawn;
Curates, long dust, will come and go
On lissom, clerical, printless toe;
And oft between the boughs is seen
The sly shade of a Rural Dean . . .
Till, at a shiver in the skies,
Vanishing with Satanic cries,
The prim ecclesiastic rout
Leaves but a startled sleeper-out,
Grey heavens, the first bird's drowsy calls,
The falling house that never falls.

God! I will pack, and take a train,
And get me to England once again!
For England's the one land, I know,
Where men with Splendid Hearts may go;

And Cambridgeshire, of all England,
The shire for Men who Understand;
And of *that* district I prefer
The lovely hamlet Grantchester.
For Cambridge people rarely smile,
Being urban, squat, and packed with guile;
And Royston men in the far South
Are black and fierce and strange of mouth;
At Over they fling oaths at one,
And worse than oaths at Trumpington,
And Ditton girls are mean and dirty,
And there's none in Harston under thirty,
And folks in Shelford and those parts
Have twisted lips and twisted hearts,
And Barton men make Cockney rhymes,
And Coton's full of nameless crimes,
And things are done you'd not believe
At Madingley, on Christmas Eve.
Strong men have run for miles and miles,
When one from Cherry Hinton smiles;

Strong men have blanched, and shot their wives,
Rather than send them to St Ives;
Strong men have cried like babes, bydam,
To hear what happened at Babraham.
But Grantchester! ah, Grantchester!
There's peace and holy quiet there,
Great clouds along pacific skies,

And men and women with straight eyes,
Lithe children lovelier than a dream,
A bosky wood, a slumbrous stream,
And little kindly winds that creep
Round twilight corners, half asleep.
In Grantchester their skins are white;
They bathe by day, they bathe by night;
The women there do all they ought;
The men observe the Rules of Thought.
They love the Good; they worship Truth;
They laugh uproariously in youth;
(And when they get to feeling old,
They up and shoot themselves, I'm told) . . .

Ah God! to see the branches stir
Across the moon at Grantchester!
To smell the thrilling-sweet and rotten
Unforgettable, unforgotten
River-smell, and hear the breeze
Sobbing in the little trees.
Say, do the elm-clumps greatly stand
Still guardians of that holy land?
The chestnuts shade, in reverend dream,
The yet unacademic stream?
Is dawn a secret shy and cold
Anadyomene, silver-gold?
And sunset still a golden sea
From Haslingfield to Madingley?
And after, ere the night is born,

Do hares come out about the corn?
Oh, is the water sweet and cool,
Gentle and brown, above the pool?
And laughs the immortal river still
Under the mill, under the mill?
Say, is there Beauty yet to find?
And Certainty? and Quiet kind?
Deep meadows yet, for to forget
The lies, and truths, and pain? . . . Oh! yet
Stands the Church clock at ten to three?
And is there honey still for tea?

## Travel

'Twas when I was in Neu Strelitz
I broke my heart in little bits.

So while I sat in the Müritz train
I glued the bits together again.

But when I got to Amerhold,
I felt the glue would never hold.

And now that I'm home to Barton Hill,
I know once broken is broken still.

## In Freiburg Station

In Freiburg station, waiting for a train,
I saw a Bishop in puce gloves go by.
Now God may thunder furious from the sky,
Shattering all my glory into pain,
And joy turn stinking rotten, hope be vain,
Night fall on little laughters, little loves,
And better Bishops don more glorious gloves,
While I go down in darkness; what care I?

There is one memory God can never break,
There is one splendour more than all the pain,
There is one secret that shall never die,
Star-crowned I stand and sing, for that hour's sake.
In Freiburg station, waiting for a train,
I saw a Bishop with puce gloves go by.

## The Fish

In a cool curving world he lies
And ripples with dark ecstasies.
The kind luxurious lapse and steal
Shapes all his universe to feel
And know and be; the clinging stream
Closes his memory, glooms his dream,
Who lips the roots o' the shore, and glides
Superb on unreturning tides.
Those silent waters weave for him
A fluctuant mutable world and dim,
Where wavering masses bulge and gape
Mysterious, and shape to shape
Dies momently through whorl and hollow,
And form and line and solid follow
Solid and line and form to dream
Fantastic down the eternal stream;
An obscure world, a shifting world,
Bulbous, or pulled to thin, or curled,
Or serpentine, or driving arrows,
Or serene slidings, or March narrows.
There slipping wave and shore are one,
And weed and mud. No ray of sun,
But glow to glow fades down the deep

(As dream to unknown dream in sleep);
Shaken translucency illumes
The hyaline of drifting glooms;
The strange soft-handed depth subdues
Drowned colour there, but black to hues,
As death to living, decomposes –
Red darkness of the heart of roses,
Blue brilliant from dead starless skies,
And gold that lies behind the eyes,
The unknown unnameable sightless white
That is the essential flame of night,
Lustreless purple, hooded green,
The myriad hues that lie between
Darkness and darkness! . . .

                    And all's one
Gentle, embracing, quiet, dun,
The world he rests in, world he knows,
Perpetual curving. Only – grows
An eddy in that ordered falling,
A knowledge from the gloom, a calling
Weed in the wave, gleam in the mud –
The dark fire leaps along his blood;
Dateless and deathless, blind and still,
The intricate impulse works its will;
His woven world drops back; and he,

Sans providence, sans memory,
Unconscious and directly driven,
Fades to some dank sufficient heaven.

O world of lips, O world of laughter,
Where hope is fleet and thought flies after,
Of lights in the clear night, of cries
That drift along the wave and rise
Thin to the glittering stars above,
You know the hands, the eyes of love!
The strife of limbs, the sightless clinging
The infinite distance, and the singing
Blown by the wind, a flame of sound,
The gleam, the flowers, and vast around
The horizon, and the heights above –
You know the sigh, the song of love!

But there the night is close, and there
Darkness is cold and strange and bare;
And the secret deeps are whisperless;
And rhythm is all deliciousness;
And joy is in the throbbing tide,
Whose intricate fingers beat and glide
In felt bewildering harmonies
Of trembling touch; and music is
The exquisite knocking of the blood.
Space is no more, under the mud;

His bliss is older than the sun.
Silent and straight the waters run.
The lights, the cries, the willows dim,
And the dark tide are one with him.

## *Colloquial*

It was not that you said I thought you knew,
Or that you thought I said that you, my dear,
Felt what I felt you felt. If it were clear,
Had God given soul to me, or sense to you,
Or guts, indeed, to either of the two,
Had it been worth a smile, or worth a tear,
Heart of my heart.

## A *Letter to a Live Poet*

Sir, since the last Elizabethan died,
Or, rather, that more Paradisal muse,
Blind with much light, passed to the light more glorious
Or deeper blindness, no man's hand, as thine,
Has, on the world's most noblest chord of song,
Struck certain magic strains. Ears satiate
With the clamorous, timorous whisperings of today,
Thrilled to perceive once more the spacious voice
And serene utterance of old. We heard
– With rapturous breath half-held, as a dreamer dreams
Who dares not know it dreaming, lest he wake –
The odorous, amorous style of poetry,
The melancholy knocking of those lines,
The long, low soughing of pentameters,
– Or the sharp of rhyme as a bird's cry –
And the innumerable truant polysyllables
Multitudinously twittering like a bee.
Fulfilled our hearts were with that music then,
And all the evenings sighed it to the dawn,
And all the lovers heard it from all the trees.
All of the accents upon all the norms!
– And ah! the stress on the penultimate!
We never knew blank verse could have such feet.

Where is it now? Oh, more than ever, now
I sometimes think no poetry is read
Save where some sepultured Cæsura bled,
Royally incarnadining all the line.
Is the imperial iamb laid to rest,
And the young trochee, having done enough?
Ah! turn again! Sing so to us, who are sick
Of seeming-simple rhymes, bizarre emotions,
Decked in the simple verses of the day,
Infinite meaning in a little gloom,
Irregular thoughts in stanzas regular,
Modern despair in antique metres, myths
Incomprehensible at evening,
And symbols that mean nothing in the dawn.
The slow lines swell. The new style sighs. The Celt
Moans round with many voices.

                          God! to see
Gaunt anapæsts stand up out of the verse,
Combative accents, stress where no stress should be,
Spondee on spondee, iamb on choriamb,
The thrill of all the tribrachs in the world,
And all the vowels rising to the E!
To hear the blessed mutter of those verbs,
Conjunctions passionate toward each other's arms,
And epithets like amaranthine lovers
Stretching luxuriously to the stars,
All prouder pronouns than the dawn, and all
The thunder of the trumpets of the noun!

## Sonnet Reversed

Hand trembling towards hand; the amazing lights
Of heart and eye. They stood on supreme heights.

Ah, the delirious weeks of honeymoon!
  Soon they returned, and, after strange adventures,
Settled at Balham by the end of June.
  Their money was in Can. Pacs. B. Debentures,
And in Antofagastas. Still he went
  Cityward daily; still she did abide
At home. And both were really quite content
  With work and social pleasures. Then they died.
They left three children (besides George, who drank):
  The eldest Jane, who married Mr Bell,
William, the head-clerk in the County Bank,
  And Henry, a stock-broker, doing well.

## Sonnet

Oh! Death will find me, long before I tire
    Of watching you; and swing me suddenly
Into the shade and loneliness and mire
    Of the last land! There, waiting patiently,

One day, I think, I'll feel a cool wind blowing,
    See a slow light across the Stygian tide,
And hear the Dead about me stir, unknowing,
    And tremble. And *I* shall know that you have died,

And watch you, a broad-browed and smiling dream,
    Pass, light as ever, through the lightless host,
Quietly ponder, start, and sway, and gleam –
    Most individual and bewildering ghost! –

And turn, and toss your brown delightful head
Amusedly, among the ancient Dead.

## Failure

Because God put His adamantine fate
    Between my sullen heart and its desire,
I swore that I would burst the Iron Gate,
    Rise up, and curse Him on His throne of fire.
Earth shuddered at my crown of blasphemy,
    But Love was as a flame about my feet;
    Proud up the Golden Stair I strode; and beat
Thrice on the Gate, and entered with a cry –

All the great courts were quiet in the sun,
    And full of vacant echoes: moss had grown
Over the glassy pavement, and begun
    To creep within the dusty council-halls.
An idle wind blew round an empty throne
    And stirred the heavy curtains on the walls.

# A Note on Rupert Brooke

Rupert Chawner Brooke (1887–1915), English poet, born at Rugby, where his father was a housemaster at the school. From there he went to King's College, Cambridge. He settled at the Old Vicarage, Grantchester, subject of one of his most famous poems, and numbered among his friends Edward Marsh, Gosse, Drinkwater, de la Mare, W. W. Gibson, W. H. Davies, and the Asquiths. In 1911 he was made a fellow of King's, published a small volume of poems, and planned the anthology *Georgian Poetry* with Harold Monro.

In 1913 he travelled widely, crossing America and going on to Hawaii, Samoa, Fiji and Tahiti, but his plans were interrupted by the First World War. Commissioned in 1914 he was with the Royal Naval Division at Antwerp, and in 1915 was sent to the Dardanelles, but died of septicaemia in Scyros, the fabled island of Achilles, where he was buried.

Brooke's poems won great fame, both because the war sonnets in the posthumous volume *1914 and Other Poems*, 1915, caught the prevailing early wartime spirit of splendid and selfless patriotism, and because he himself typified the generation of young men which was being ruthlessly sacrificed in the 'war to end wars'.